Common Thread Of Women

"Putting love into perspective"

By Nina Dean

Common Thread of Women
"Putting love into persepective"

Text Copyright & Illustrations Copyright -2007 by Nina Dean
Nia Faith Publishing of Bolingbrook Illinois

ISBN #978-0-9801163-0-4

All the stories related in this book are loosely based on actual events, but has been altered to protect any woman's pain or shame. These stories are shared to let some women know that they are not alone. These stories can let some men know the kind of pain, they can inflict in a relationship. The goal is to protect and respect the privacy of anyone who shared their stories with me. Some stories were from people that were met over the course of my lifetime on a bus stop, on a train ride, in a grocery store, etc. They cannot be located nor can the names be remembered. There stories never died in my memory because of the experience that landed on my doorstep with the Bo Bo in my life. At that moment of reflection, the common thread was discovered between women for me.

Scripture references were from experience of growing up in church. The experiences were from the thousands of sermons that were heard in the course of my church attendance. The Biblical stories and experience came from a lifetime of reading many Bibles including the KJV and New International Version.

All rights reserved. No portion of this book may be reproduced in any form without written permission of Nina Dean of Nia Faith Publishing.

Printed in the United States of America

Printed by Brio Print, Minneapolis, MN 55416

Dedication

This book is dedicated to my husband and our four sons. It is also a dedication to the memory of my grandmother Lilly Mae Hamilton who helped mold and shape me. My grandmother had a way with words and wisdom well beyond my years. She helped ease my fears and lessen my tears. Also, this book is dedicated to the memory of my father-in-law, Joe Sr. He was the legacy that created a generation of men in my life. I debated the philosophies of life with him. He would give me advice on how to stay married and raise four sons. The much needed advice is missed but he is not forgotten.

Acknowledgements

I would like to thank God for sending me down as one of his messengers. I may not have always delivered his message the way that he wanted me to. I delivered it in my humanness and brokenness. Thank you, God for being sovereign and never giving up on me. I am thankful to you Lord for sparing my life on September 26, 2005 through Dr. Josupait and staff. When my chances were grave you raised me up for your glory.

Thanks to my husband, Joe. Joe and I have been together through most of life's stages since we met when I was six and he was eight. We are trying to learn to stop fighting each other and to fight for the future of our four intelligent, strong and valiant sons; Jovontae, Nolan, Jayden and Nehemiah. Joe, you have challenged me to raise the bar in life through methods that I could not understand nor explain. I am thankful that we have kept pressing forward in spite of all obstacles and life tests.

Thanks to my sons, they are my true motivation. The future is going to be brighter because these four boys were chosen by God and sent through my husband's seed and my womb to do great work in the vineyards. I love you Dean Boys. You guys have created precious memories for your Dad and me. Thank you for loving us and helping us realize that dreams do come true. Thanks for being a source of strength for Dad and I to keep on going. Do know that you have parents that are behind you, in front of you and beside you.

Thanks to my parents Johnny and Peggy Jordan. Thanks for

raising me and my siblings; Loyce, Myosia and Johnny Jr. the best way you knew how. Thanks for keeping us in your arms and in the hands of the Lord. We know that God hears your prayers. Thanks for you showing us God's mercy and grace.

Thanks to all my special friends and aunts, you know who you are. Thanks to all my friends and extended family. I cannot list all of you, but if you have my phone number and use it, then that means you. Thank you all for your love and encouragement to push ahead in some of my darkest days. Thanks for your unconditional and agape love. Much love and thanks to the seeds of Joe and Lilly Mae Hamilton of Marianna, Arkansas. Please accept my kisses for all of you.

Love and thanks, Nina D

The Company of A M A N

Some Women feel they need the company of a man
They take beatings, disrespect, broken hearts and unfinished dreams
Just for the company of a man

Some women bear children and struggle to raise them alone
Some loss sight of origin, dropping their once held high heads
Just for the company of a man

Some women allow their children to be raped and molested by their man
They will do jail time, deteriorate and die
Just for the company of a man

Some Women degrade themselves by being men sex slaves
They allow their insides to be destroyed from the sex abuse
Just for the company of a man

Have they ever stopped and dug deep into their souls
Who conceived man, who carried man, who gave birth to man, who raised man?

W O M A N
Wake up my, Sista

Contents

Chapter 1: What are you up against?

Chapter 2: How did you get here?

Chapter 3: Did something happen in the Garden of Eden?

Chapter 4: Who wants Bo Bo, anyway?

Chapter 5: God's vengeance or my revenge?

Chapter 6: Sista you are not alone

Chapter 7: Is this your story?

Chapter 8: Help me Holy Spirit!

Chapter 9: My Violations; His victories

Chapter 10: Stop cell phone checking and drive bys

Chapter 11: Breaking away from Bo Bo

Chapter 12: Adjustment/Alignment

Chapter 13: Sista Soar and change you!!!

Chapter 14: Understand and forge ahead, create the NEW

Chapter One

WHAT ARE YOU UP AGAINST?

The Common Thread of Women is often men. If you ask women to talk about their life, I would say that men would be at the top of the list. Companionship and relationships are a big part of a woman's life. It seems that the topic of men crosses all racial and class divides. The topic of men seems to unite women into a sisterhood creating their common thread. It is quite amazing how you can close your eyes in a room full of women and listen to what is shared and it would seem as if your story is being told by some one else in the room. You will hear that you are mirror images of each other.

The issues, problems and stories may vary from one extreme to the other but, if you listen closely, the common thread begins to unravel itself so you can identify the thread that is shared. Somehow women are tightly connected by the thread of life. The thread may be the men one used to sew the initial stitch or it can be the loop that binds the entire project together. One thread that women often share is being able to trust men.

When the trust is violated between women and men, the pain is a threaded connection for women. The pain of coping and living through the violations is real and intensive. The connection is real and it seems to be on display like a badge on a general's uniform in the armed forces. Some women are more wounded than others and may have more war wounds that are displayed. The wounds are not intended for public display. It is revealed no matter how hard you try to conceal the pain.

We refer to the Word of God regarding trust. God tells us to trust no men because they will fail you every time. Living in today's world is such a task. The Word refers to the trials and tribulations as spiritual warfare. We are constantly fighting against principalities and darkness. As a woman and after speaking to many women of different generations, I am convinced that we can trust no men. God has already revealed this in his word that our trust belongs in him.

The Word of God clearly states that women were put here to help men. From the beginning of time, women have multitasked and this gift is evident. It is also a coping mechanism that gets women through. The Lord placed women in a supporting role which holds all things together. Women take what is given and produce at all cost. Sometimes I wonder why there is so much responsibility on the woman when the men are to lead the family. I am confident that God makes no mistakes and the roles of women are part of God's plan.

As women we have a unique make up, we are emotional and nurturing at the same time. The church is filled with our presence because we suffer many silent pains and our faith is in God for emotional deliverance. Many women seek deliverance from a broken relationship, not the hardship or stress of being a
W O M A N.

Many of us have broken hearts and open wounds that salt often finds its way in over and over again. The salt is Satan's way of trying to keep us emotionally bound and which destroys us. On the salt days we thank God for our girlfriends and confidantes that we pour our heart out to regardless of our struggles with men and the pain in our lives.

The girlfriends are our counselors, friends, spiritual prayer partners, encouragers and motivation. When we pour out our hearts and receive good advice and understand that we were understood, it feels like salvation over again. In a woman's life only God and girlfriends brings us comfort. It is truly a blessing that we can open up about the secrets that haunts us in our sleep. Breaking the silence goes against what we are told. Men tell us what goes on in the home stays in the home. The men brainwash us because they do not want to be known as the predator that they are. They hide behind their mask to avoid public scrutiny.

Common Thread Of Women

Over the years after meeting many women, I have learned that inside we are all the same. We are looking for similar things to satisfy and put the raging fires out inside of us. As women we want peace in our homes, we want that near perfect God fearing man, and to have love and appreciation for some of the roles that we play with unconditional love. Conditions have been placed on us since the beginning of time and the test never stops. Our men may leave us even if we meet their demands. We try hard to keep it together to keep the men even if he is a piece or a fragment of a man. Some of us think, having a piece of a man that is physically, verbally or mentally abusive is better than no man at all.

Inside we know that staying with a piece of a man is not best but it beats being alone. The appearance of a relationship looks good like the peacock. All we need to endure with him is to keep girlfriends on speed dial to help us with the psychosis. In the end we know that he is not right and cannot be apart of God's plan but we counsel with friends and pray for brighter days. In our mind we pull out the scale to see if the relationship balances or rationalizes why we stay with "Bo Bo". "Bo Bo" is broken and needs God's direction and therefore he will not stay with us and love us no matter if all his conditions are met.

"Bo Bo" not staying has nothing to do with you; it's who he is or not. The Bible refers to him as a double minded man and unstable in all his ways. Therefore, how can we meet his conditions if they change according to the weather or time? If he does not know his own self how can he know what his conditions to adhere by are. He should be lead by the Word of God and love you like Christ loves the church. This goes back to what we must hold fast in our mind, trust no men because they always fail. Our healing and mental deliverance has to come from above. This world is full of broken people as well as the church. Broken people do not want to be broken, so some of them seek help in the local church hospital. The church is a hospital for us who are emotionally sick and radiated with pain and problems. Pain and problems can lead to many different types of illness. Nothing in our up bringing prepares us for this type of darkness.

Common Thread Of Women

Masking our pain can be so overwhelming. We cry out to God in order to breathe and make it through the day. As women we have menstrual from early on, we have to carry our babies in our wombs for nine months each time and carry them in our hearts for life. In the meantime we are trying to maintain a relationship with "Bo Bo" even if it is not healthy but it is a " R E L A T I O N S H I P " . Test and trials come our way and we solve most and make adjustments for the rest. Positive results are achieved through the fruits of our labor. When it comes to "Bo Bo", it is a story within a story. He makes you love and hate him at the same time. Ultimately, after years of enduring his madness you want to throw your hands up. Yet we pray and believe that all things are possible through Christ, even for "Bo Bo".

We read all the books, listen to the tapes and try to get all the self help that we can to make it through our emotional pain and wreckage. We watch our boys and girls witness our madness only to repeat our actions for generations to come. We let generational curses begin because we love "Bo Bo", well the piece that we have. "Bo Bo" feels void and pain because he does not love you like Christ loves the church because he does not know Christ intimately.

Look at "Bo Bo" now, girl, he is cheating. How can he do this? He is only a piece of man and has hurt me all over. What have I done to deserve this? God, are you there? Why me Lord, this is my girlfriend's story, not mine. This was not to be me, why did this fall on my door step? Like I do not have enough things to manage; borderline losing my religion Lord, I need you RIGHT NOW, GOD! Lord, I deal with the hurts and all the burdens that come along with "Bo Bo" such as him not having a father and if he had one he was an alcoholic. He was present in "Bo Bo's" home but absent, he smoked weed on top of that, he had trouble with the law, his mother did not direct him but accepted him whether good or bad, he cannot find or keep a job, his abuse, his lack of encouragement and now "Nay Nay" is messing with my man.

Enough is enough. I need to run and hide, but my children need me and my job is needed to keep a roof over our heads. Lord, should I be grateful that it is "Nay Nay" and not "Tyrone". Because you know that the down low has come out of the closet. What am I thinking, it is okay as long as it is a woman with my man instead of a man with my man, God have mercy.

This new age devil is clearly more potent and harder to detect. It is written in revelations that men would become lovers of themselves. Lord, this cannot be a battle that I can win. Going back to your Word Lord, you said that I am more than a conquer and the battle is not mine, it is yours.

Clearly, I need to pull out my self help tapes from T D Jakes to learn how to fight for this family. On second thought, why do I have to fight for the family when the family is not fighting for me? Too many obstacles and not enough time or strength in this lifetime; Lord, I am wounded and bathing in salt with my hands thrown up and deliverance does not seem near or even conceivable.

The joy of the Lord is my strength according to the Bible; I have neither joy nor strength. The bills are due; I have a meeting at church and a parent teacher conference at my kids' school. Needless to say, my personal needs are not met. I would love to complete the tasks at hand and go home to slide into a Calgone bath to really see if it takes me away as the commercial states. My bed will be empty and if Bo Bo is there he is probably exhausted from Nay Nay. Nay Nay goes places that are erotic and that has to be a sin. Cell phones and pagers have ruined many marriages and relationships today because it makes extra marital affairs easy. The technology is more than a notion. To top it off, not only are the other women performing oral sex, these women are blowing and licking men between the cheeks. How can good girls compete with such perversion? The new age devil has convinced Bo Bo that he is everything for those few hours beyond his countless faults. See, Bo Bo does not have to help her pay bills or help with her children. She is not tired from washing his clothes and preparing his meals.

Bo Bo wants Lisa Ray and the lady with the Tina Turner legs without seeing the preparation that went into the Hollywood manufactured look. He wants you to go to bed as Beyonce and wake up as Beyonce. He wants you to not smell like the chicken you just fried or have a form of exhaustion from running from the cleaners for his clothes, the store for his meal, to school for his kids or the post office to mail the bills. He wants you to smell so fresh and have the ability to maintain sweet breathe with no tooth brush. Then he has the nerve to want you to simulate his mind, body and his soul without considering maybe you need a massage or sweet nothing in your ear. Did he forget the 52 hours you spent on the job outside the home not including the 100 plus hours at home? No consideration is given for the kids' good grades and the positive results in their extra curricular activities. No consideration for dinner on the table in some shape or form seven days a week. No appreciation for homemade corn bread but jiffy mix is his hearts delight. How much can one take and how did you get here?

Chapter *Two*

How did you get here?

You got here by force and had no choice. This sounds correct because you was born a **W O M A N**. With this gender selection comes many roles, responsibilities, obligations and titles. Some of the adjectives that men have given to women are demeaning and degrading. Some of the adjectives have been communicated to the world through rap songs. It is very intriguing how men can play "catch a girl, kiss a girl" when young, then later in life catch a case for hitting a girl. As women we were taught about appearances early on and how to play roles of many.

Depending on the place or occasion we were taught about impromptu acting and how to stage the performance of a lifetime. We were taught to bring in the ranks and not question it. Fake it until you make it girl. Fake it in bed if Bo Bo is not that good because he has to feel like a man even if you never have an orgasm. Fake it out of bed or they will discover that you are broken and not whole. Being broken is not part of a woman because we were designed to be a completer. We are to complete that piece of a man's inadequate conception of a master piece.

Did I get here from the coat room in school where Bo Bo took me to feel me up and slap me for not liking it? Every other girl is liked by Bo Bo so I should be excited that it is me on his mind today. Even if I feel misused, my role is to please others and pretend everything is all right. Mom never told me about Bo Bo even though she sleeps with him every night. Why would our mothers who love us so much let us meet Bo Bo and think that he constitutes love? Where was the warning and if she did warn us why did we not listen?

Really, how many Bo Bos are there out there? Well, I have counted every woman I have had the privilege of knowing and all I hear is story after story, pain after pain, hopefulness for the hopeless, trial after tribulation , oh God the thoughts remind me that I need salvation.

I wonder is it better to marry than to burn. Bo Bo makes me feel that I am charred inside and out. Does the fire not count? Bo Bo brings a new meaning to it is getting hot in here. If this relationship makes me feel so hot can hell be less intense? Hell on earth then Hell after death, when does the heat stop? I will settle for Texas at the hottest point instead of this desert that is deserted. In the desert you can find the camels and me with no water in sight.

I wish that Psalms 23 worked for me. I feel the valley of the shadow of death as I walk, I do fear evil and Bo Bo's wrath. I trust and believe that God knew that Bo Bo existed when David wrote this Psalm. Was there another avenue, street, place, court or circle that I could have detoured on because I need to go back and start all over again. Oh wait, I cannot start over again because I have three kids living not including the five that were aborted because Bo Bo could not take the noise and additional pressures. What about the extra fifty pounds that I carry? What about the inside scars that convince me that Bo Bo is all right? How did I get here? Can I tap my heels three times and go home? Can I keep the glass slippers past midnight? Can faith of a mustard seed remove Bo Bo and the pieces he has left in me? Help, I would like to drink and dance my pains and troubles away. I cannot do this because if I get lost how do my children find me. I want to go the heaven and have peace with the Lord. Can I throw my thoughts into the sea of forgetfulness?

Chapter Three

Did something happen in the Garden of Eden?

$\mathcal{B}$o Bo has an affect on me and it affects everything I do. Being consumed with his madness is a constant battle in my mind. Does Bo Bo spend as much time as I do telling the story and trying to deal with the issues in our relationship? God only created men and women so life should not seem as a constant battle ground? Was life not meant to be better than this or did I choose the wrong Bo Bo? Let's take a look at the Garden of Eden where it all began to see how this started. Did Adam and Eve have this much trouble? Can I trace Bo Bo back to the beginning or should I begin over without him, which sounds like the path of the least resistance?

In the beginning of mankind God created Adam and Eve. They were husband and wife and the first to exist. Sin entered into the world because Satan deceived the woman and Adam followed her lead. Adam blamed his wife for him eating from the tree of knowledge which led to sin. Satan has been around from the beginning of time trying to win souls from Christ. Adam was deceived by his wife and the result was catastrophic. It changed mankind forever and opened it up to evil. Free will was given to each of us and the acceptance of Christ is a choice. Constantly tested by evil and told to resist by the Lord, is where we are currently.

The foundation has laid Bo Bo a hard road ahead because from the beginning man did not take a stand but yielded to sin through his wife. Today, Bo Bo is not taking a stand and is deceived by women and the promises of their "Jewels". First, it is Nay Nay, then SheNeeda because his flesh is never content nor his desires because his focus is not God and if he says that it is he is being mislead. Bo Bo starts out with Nay Nay, the round the way girl because she is exciting and new. Then, here is his favorite SheNeeda. She **Need** A this and A that. She needs everything and Bo Bo wants to feel needed. Supplying SheNeeda needs is not his goal because truly Bo Bo cannot. She enjoys his empty company because she has a void. SheNeeda does not care if he is married or if she is one of many. SheNeeda fools herself daily and feels lower than low. She likes to hear the lies and believe that they are true. She is looking for love and just a humanly image of a male that lights up her eyes. SheNeeda never complains. She sends him home on time every night with a kiss and will drive him home if he needs a ride.

SheNeeda is a woman with low self esteem and feels neglected and has no way to know or express her emotional distress. SheNeeda knows the wife's name and has lain in their bed when she was in the hospital having Bo Bo's child and feels no shame. SheNeeda is silent and has no demands. She is Bo Bo's biggest cheerleader and always available at his command. She will stop what she is doing because she wants to give Bo Bo her all. Her mother will keep her kids so it will not aggravate Bo Bo. Her mother encourages her relationship with this married man. See SheNeeda's mother never could keep a man. SheNeeda will spend all of her welfare check and part time pay, just to stay out and play with Bo Bo. She will later borrow what she needs for her and the children. She feels that she needs a man in a fragment of her life. SheNeeda can go without hearing from Bo Bo for months and will not question the space. She will just pick up from where they left off. She is grateful that Bo Bo comes back to share a moment with her.

He can do this for years and years and she will not cry a tear. She does not care if he ever divorces or if he divorces and marries someone other than her, it is all good to her. SheNeeda understands that the choices he makes are not hers but his. He is in control and she stays in her place neatly tucked away. Bo Bo knows that she will never go anywhere. He can convince his wife that a woman will not put up with his in and out moves. This would leave the wife to think well, I do not have to worry about that one. In reality, she does because if Bo Bo never sees her again it will be because he is delivered. The other women will accept Bo Bo whenever and however. Bo Bo continues to run the race and knows that his empty words will keep SheNeeda convinced that she needs a part of him. See, Nay Nay may trip because she thinks he will one day leave his wife but not SheNeeda.

SheNeeda never had a father in her life. She has only one photo of her father and has only seen him twice. She never stopped loving him or telling her peers about the two experiences she had with him. She neglects to let the story reflect that this was only two encounters. She tells the stories that seem so complete as if he was right there in her life. She never gave up Daddy's space in her heart. She has created her own reality in her mind. This puts her Dad totally there in her reality. SheNeeda never questioned his absence but keeps the fond memories in her mind to fill the space and knows when he returns it will be okay. She never cried or asked why he left for long periods of time. Her love for him keeps her pressing forward. The two visits that her Dad shared with her were wonderful even though on the second one he asked her for money. She was happy to see him and would have given all that she had because she felt excited inside. SheNeeda never got her hopes up or anticipated his next showing but yet she kept glowing. Therefore, meeting a Bo Bo gives her the same feelings that she has concerning her father. She thinks that the Bo Bo behavior is the norm. She could let Bo Bo come and goes as he pleased because she had that glow. She will accept him if and when he returns.

SheNeeda never envied her friends who have wonderful dads because the two times her Dad came by were so wonderful. She would reflect and equate their joy with hers. Bo Bo never leaving his wife or any of the others does not matter because she knows her place and had never had an established relationship with a parental male figure. She thinks this is how men pretty much operate. SheNeeda has children that never see stability and never see their mother's heart because she missed out or was never introduced to any other type of life. She cannot pass on something that she has not seen. She could learn best if she let God be her father and guide her into the fullness of life in Christ.

Christ in his abundance would be the solution for SheNeeda because only God can heal her broken heart. In the beginning we broke God's heart in the Garden of Eden. We disobeyed God and opened up ourselves to deceit, cheating, lawlessness and a host of sins. Instead of trusting Satan, Eve should have trusted the Creator because he is "Trust" all by himself. In God we can find peace if we put our complete trust in him and no other. In Proverbs 3:5-7 (KJV), it says: "Trust in the Lord with all thine heart; and lean not unto thine own understanding. In all thy ways acknowledge him and he shall direct thy paths. Be not wise in thine own eyes; fear the Lord and depart from evil. "These verses show that God will direct not one path but all paths and we cannot look to ourselves for wisdom because there is no wisdom unless we are in the Lord.

SheNeeda needs the Lord and no one else because God is the only man with undeniable trust without fail. SheNeeda needs to release Bo Bo and free herself from deceit. She needs to release herself from the comfort in sin and know through God, her inadequate father/daughter relationship should not keep her in captivity to a Bo Bo because that life is not pleasing to God. When SheNeeda frees Bo Bo she frees herself to submit to God for direction because Bo Bo and she are lost and out of touch from God. If Bo Bo was not lost he would not need SheNeeda in his life or any of the others. He would not continue to hurt his wife and children through adultery.

Now, let's take a look at why Nay Nay loves Bo Bo. She is an around the way girl that loves to have fun and has engaged in things you cannot imagine. She loves life and will keep the party going even if the Disc Jockey has left the building. She thrives on excitement and thrill and the edge is not far enough. Nay Nay loves to fall off and see what happens. As long as Nay Nay wakes up it is a new opportunity to seize another part of what life owes her because she states that when she dies "she swears the world will owe her nothing". Nay Nay loves Bo Bo and whoever else she meets that week. Nay Nay does not want to know the rules and if you show them to her she will be determined to break everyone. Nay Nay is bad and wants men to know it. She will try whatever has been tried and take the dare on what he can imagine. She is proud of her ability to make men cry in bed and call her name. She will take the men from under you and ask him to meet her in the men's rest room of any establishment. She takes pleasure in being a bad girl and loves to brag about it. Nay Nay's Daddy is the local ladies man. Her mother is never with the same man.

Nay Nay feels that you would want to see her because she is very erotic and does things your wife will never consider or heard about. She wants you to take her to the mall and pay for her some new shoes when you get paid. She will tell your wife, if you get out of control. She will put the sugar in the tank and show up at your front door just to let the Mrs. know that Bo Bo is "OUR" man. She thrives on drama and she got it from her mama. She is not afraid of dumping Bo Bo but Bo Bo is not going to let her go that easy because she is worth her weight in gold because she has many positions and stories untold.

Nay Nay is a man's visual delight and she delivers every time. She never wants to fuss and fight, only make love all through the night. She will grant Bo Bo's wish like a genie in the bottle and then say is that all you got. She is fire and leaves the guns smoking. She has a night stand full of antibiotics and can diagnose herself instead of going to the clinic. She will risk it all because that is her high. All I say is that Nay Nay needs JESUS with the capital J. She needs deliverance from her flesh and needs to leave all the Bo Bos and Bobbies alone. She has made her way around the world and she is on her way back. Lord, knows once was enough for the world. Nay Nay needs to find joy and strength in Lord.

Chapter *Four*

WHO WANTS A BO BO, ANYWAY?

*B*affled and confused, Bo Bo's wife is asking the questions, playing detective with Bo Bo to investigate who wants him with all his issues and a wife. She cries and prays, searched and discovers who wants Bo Bo. She knows that the world is made up of many different people and no two people may respond the same way. It has been brought to light that Nay Nay and SheNeeda are sleeping with her husband. This is very painful and very complex because in the word of God the two has become one. Husbands and wives are one in the same (one flesh). Therefore, this explains why Bo Bo's effect on his wife goes deeper than the physical, it is spiritual and mental. The covenant that was made before God makes two, one. The Word tells the husband to leave his father and mother and cleave to his wife. The Word says what God has joined together let no man put them under.

The wife asks who wants Bo Bo and why does he not want me, I am his wife. The wife wrestles with the marriage and questions why they got married, if they did not want to be committed. Who wants Bo Bo is relatively easy to Satan. A part of the curse on men is inadequacy. He uses women to entice Bo Bo because the curse on him is closely tied to inadequacy. Adam followed Eve and that was not how it was designed. The work that was once easy is labor intensive for men as a result of the fall in the Garden of Eden. Men may choose not to deal with the problems or concerns in his life or marriage because he does not want to face possible disappointment. Men want to protect their masculinity at all cost, even if the cost is sin. Men will hide and seek protection in other women, if their wife is too verbally expressive. They may abuse her physically or mentally and wear her down over time. The whole demonic spirit is psychological. The battle between men and women creates an outlet for men not to face his problems at home. He avoids his wife and it can lead to adultery. A man would not sin if he did not find pleasure in it. He would not cheat on his spouse if he felt fulfillment.

Marriage is a work in progress and the devil is a deceiver. He wants you to feel void so he can use you for his purposes. When feelings of discontentment, anger or inadequacy comes up in a marriage, you have to lean to the Word of God to hear what God thinks. You have to labor with the family because God will reward. Bo Bo, retreating to Nay Nay or SheNeeda only creates a complex situation for the family. The women that the men use outside the marriage are already broken. If the other women were not broken they would not lay with other people's husbands. Nor would women lay with men who will not commit to them whole heartedly. Sex is an action and you can not stock up on it, it is ongoing intimacy that should be enjoyed according to God's Word and design. Why do other women want your husband is because Satan wants to destroy the family. Destroying the family gives him room to work with each individual. Satan does not want to fight the strength of the family as a unit that is much too powerful for him. Together the family has more power and God's protection which weighs on the devil's ability to destroy.

Truly, the other woman does not want your man, they want one of their own but sin has taught them to settle. When the other woman breaks free and stops messing with your husband, she may want a husband of her own. Then she will have to pay God's price for her sin. The Word says you reap what you sow. It seems clear that the reaping process is true when it comes to you. However, it never seems as if the husband actually pays for his sins. When the husband cheats, it causes all kind of pain in your life and the children's lives. The pain cannot be described and has a relentless effect on your whole being. It seems it should be something you can do to help God repay Bo Bo for his wrong to you. Bo Bo has sent you through enough to last two lifetimes and may even three. You think you can help God out with the big payback with Bo Bo. He is lying next to you and seems to have no worry in this whole world. You are full of emotion and rage from the storm that appears to have passed. You want Bo Bo to be on the other side of the storm and feel your pain to the highest power imaginable. Now, you want to put God on the shelf, so you can take matters in your own hands. It is payback time and you believe it begins Right Now!

Chapter Five

God's Vengence or My Revenge?

Trust by definition means to place your confidence in, to hope and to guard. Trust is a small word but it bears great meaning and carries tremendous responsibility. When you trust someone you do not believe that they will fail you. You have complete confidence in them. When a person violates your trust for their own personal victory it is more than complicated to work through, it can be life changing. It is hard because the person who betrays your trust has put their own selfish needs above you and has created wounds for you that you have not signed up for. The person has put you in a war that you did not enlist in, they put you in a battle that you did not want to fight and cannot find any reason that you are in the place that they have placed you in. To date, no enlistment papers with your signature are found.

When the trust is broken you feel alienated and rejected. Dealing with the pain of being violated by broken trust creates a burdened heart and many unsettling emotions. The violations weigh heavy and take you down various paths simultaneously which can lead to depression and cause you to respond out of grief and anxiety. The actions that one takes after being violated by Bo Bo are not rational but irrational to an unknown degree. You feel debilitating and hopeless. When you pour yourself into someone with unselfishness and all boundaries have been crossed, it is really painful. Intimacy is very private and personal and every experience is not the same nor can it be expressed in words. It is the opposite of love at first sight. It goes beyond the butterflies in ones stomach. The pain feels physical.

Bo Bo can view his affair as his success but it creates a sense of heart failure for the person that he cheats on. A light comes on after being a victim of an affair. Keep in mind, I never mentioned that the light was positive but it is a light just the same. Laws should be created for the victimization that one feels after such atrocity because it can create some insanity's in ones mind that can lead to a tragedy. Playing games with people's hearts has lead to death in uncountable cases. Love triangles and crime of passions started out as love at one point.

When Bo Bo creates this web of pain and has decided to break it off with the women, he is very calm. Bo Bo is too calm for you and you begin to wonder if the affair is over and if it is, you wonder why you can't find your way back to him? The affair may be over but the violated feelings that were created have not gone away. The feelings run deep inside of you and do not seem to fade away. It appears that Bo Bo can move on easily because in his mind he does not see your problem. He expresses, I am home now and I choose you this day so get over it. Then you get an idea. Hey, it is my turn to play. Let me see if I still have what it takes. You want to feel good because you are being toyed with and taken for granted. You think, there has to be a Denzel or a Tyrone out there for me who wants me too. Bo Bo does not know what he has. All the sacrifices that have been made in the relationship with him seem like a waste of time. After giving your all to Bo Bo, he walks on your back, without any remorse. That is tough. Each time that he walks over you, it gains intensity. Now look he is running you over with a Mac 10 truck, if this is gratitude, you will pass. He then turns you over to let you know that it was real and it was intentional. He is clearly arrogant and believes that this is the way of men. He wants you to deal with it because if you do not some other women will.

Unsettled in your spirit, you want the chance to see if you can drop it like it is HOT! You believe that you can work it. Those young girls better move over. You may have packed on the pounds and have a few mouths behind you to feed but you are a veteran with the capital V.

Checking out Victoria's Secret is your first move. You want to be the ground shaker and hear the words "you go girl". Any line of encouragement from another man will do because you are so wounded that even, hello lady, sounds good. It beats being called the B word (female dog) by Bo Bo. Looking for someone to hold you tight and lead you to believe that everything is all right is your mission. The new man will beg you to stay because you are on the mission to play. You will go places you have never been before with class. He will blow up your cell phone and want to give you the keys to his truck. He will call your name and make you feel no pain. Bo Bo will soon slip to the back of your mind.

Bo Bo will not have a clue that you are having this secret rendezvous because a woman can play far better than any man unless he is one of those "down low men". Two can play at that game and you will design your own game. Bo Bo will have to wonder if you are coming home on any given night. You want to get in his head and make him feel a small portion of your pain. You do not want to wait for God because his wrath seems too slow. The only thing that should be focused on is you. The right to be happy is yours and you should choose here and now. Let the games begin. The heart must be guarded; your lover can only have your body and not your mind because he is probably another Bo Bo in disguise. Once he conquers you, it will be revealed. You hate to imagine what is happening to your soul. Let's not think about God, if so you will never pay Bo Bo back. God has to understand. You can sin and ask for forgiveness later. I am sure that is what Bo Bo the preacher man does and he preaches every Sunday in some church across the great US of A. Can't one heal in their own way? Can't you find another that fills your void? Can't you lie in another's arms and not cry through the night?

Your skirts are now above your knees and you hear the voices of men calling you. Looks like you are back in the game. You need to find out some names. You must keep your composure and act sexy and luring in order to seize the moment when it comes. Your hair and nails are done and you smell like the department store's finest. You have given out your number; let's wait for the phone to ring.

"Ring, ring" as you expected. "Ring, ring", oh should you

answer? "Ring, ring", you answered and now the first date is set. The date is going well and you are in the club and he is massaging your neck. He gives you soft kisses as you hold back the tears of fear. The bill comes at the end of the evening and he asks you for ten dollars and with great disappointment, you give him twenty. You also told him to keep the change and asked him to walk you to the car because thankfully you drove. He said lets go back to my place and you share with him that this is not a good idea because at least Mr. Bo Bo at home never kept you broke. In your mind you wonder is it that bad out here that men do not pay to play. You are thinking that the man on the side has to appear better than Bo Bo so you will not feel that you have reduced your standards to a whore. This is not the goal. This is not what you imagined. You go home and not start trouble. You can make up a lie tell Bo Bo about your late arrival home tonight.

Your desire to feel whole has not been quenched. Your ill feelings for Bo Bo are intense. You call up your girlfriend and tell her the latest drama. Your girlfriend suggests that you go out with a friend of a friend. Great idea you are feeling rejuvenated. You start by finding out how your old love interest is doing. You searched high and low and bingo, you found him. He was happy to hear from you and asked you "are you ready for me after all these years?" He asked what has happened to your husband. You try to explain and it was not clear, he said he got it; you are mad at Bo Bo again and wanted some revenge. You stated to him that it was not that cut and clear. He said okay, let's meet and not play games. He wants all of the parts that you have held back for years. He started out by saying, we are adults now. I expect you to go all the way with no hesitation or reservation. He said, I will step into your game and play but it must be worth my time as well. His directness has made you ponder and you are thinking about going with the other plan.

The other plan is to have your girl hook you up with a male friend of hers. This way you can take it a little slower than with your past love interest would like. The date is set; you drive to your aunt's house to meet your blind date. You know that he is a police officer; he drives well and looks okay. He picks you up from your aunt's house and your aunt states that he looks great and she hopes you know what you are doing because this guy seems to be all together.

Your car is parked and off you go to dinner, dance and back to his place. You place a call to one of your friends to let them know where he lives. You know he is an officer but you better play it safe. His place is neat and clean, he has to be a woman's dream. You do not see any evidences of a Mrs. and his phone is not ringing off the hook. This seems promising. His conversation was great. The feet rub and back rub was straight. The compliments that he paid were over the top and by the way you kind of lost your top along the way. He rubbed you so gentle and you felt like you were melting like butter. You fell in a trance and your pants somehow fell too. He carried you to his room and you started to think, you have no birth control and you have loss control and need some help.

All you could think about was how nice this brother was to you tonight. He opened the car door for you all night. He made you walk on the inside of him and told you that he was your protector. You owe the brother something because your Bo Bo does not even do this. He said so many kind words and made you feel great. Wow, he is moving so fast and yet so slow, how do you tell him to stop? You are not a child; you are a healthy sexual adult. You are not ready for all of this, you just wanted to feel whole again and you are treading with major sin. Why must you think about sin when your deliverance through this brother is coming in now? "Ring, ring", thank God your cell phone is ringing. What a perfect opportunity to end this evening because God has given you a sign that you need to stop. You make up a story that the caller stated your daughter is sick.

Waiting on God is obviously the right thing to do so why are you taking these things in your own hands? Why do you choose to have your own plan? Fight evil with evil is no solution. All the thoughts are going through your mind as he drops you off to your car at your aunt's house. You ended the evening with a beautiful kiss. You have guilt all over you and now you must go home and face Bo Bo. You have been out all night and you know that the date's aroma is all over you. He has gotten into your spirit and has become a part of you. Being married is a spiritual commitment before God and you are in violation with God. The night was great and liberating but you know God does not see it that way. Sin surely feels good. You would never have chosen this path but it was chosen for you. You will learn and grow from this experience because you are too chicken to leave Bo Bo because you really love him. You just want him to act right and be faithful to you.

According to the Word, vengeance is the Lord; and he will repay. You cannot even go through with your attempt to pay him back by having another. The Holy Spirit is truly a reminder that you can only depend and trust God for restoration. Hard as it may seem and hard as it may be to endure, trusting God is the only refuge. Trusting him because he never fails; trusting him through the pain, tears and difficult circumstances is the only way. Choosing not to fight the battle but allowing the Lord to operate is the right choice. Putting on the full armor of Christ as he instructed will help soften the blow.

The human side wants to repay but you must know that God has the only way. More trouble and darkness will follow after we try to resolve things our way. God is looking for us to wait on him and God can change things. In the meantime, you have to be the wife and mother that you signed up to be. This is harder than words can express and it sounds unrealistic but waiting on God will later reveal what he has in store for you. Hard and as confusing as it may be, praying seems to give relief. The relief is temporary but it helps you to push on. The church, the gospel songs and the Word gives you hope that one day your trouble in this world could soon be over. How does one fight or control something beyond control. Seeking and trusting in God is what was taught. We know that this world as a whole believes in God. In chaotic times as on September 11, 2001, the nation turned to God for peace and solutions. The Bo Bo in your life is not a nation in crisis so God should be able to help.

Revenge is a double edged sword. While accomplishing your agenda through revenge, it also kills God's agenda at the same time. Meaning you want to hurt Bo Bo on one side and on the other side of the sword it hurts you because you are out of God's order. While inflicting pain, you are incurring pain in another way. It seems to be an endless process of pain. It is clear in life that what goes around comes around. Revenge keeps the circle of pay back coming and never halting. Unfortunately, it seems that women have to stop and trust God without trying to vindicate themselves through vengeful mean. The stakes are high when you take paying Bo Bo back in your own way. What Bo Bo does wrong will be paid to him by God. If you pay him back, you must also pay. The revenge cycle is ongoing and that is why God must pay what is due not you.

Chapter Six

SISTA YOU ARE NOT ALONE

$\mathcal{S}$ista, your story is not isolated, uncommon, foreign, embarrassing, strange, unheard of nor unable to fathom. This story has been told from generations past until the present. The women's name changes from story to story. They live in different places and of many different races. This is common, real and painful. It seems that the Bo Bo of our life is the only constant or guarantee in the story. It seems that Bo Bo should be satisfied with one woman and treat her well. It seems as if Bo Bo should want to raise a family with his dedicated wife. He should be proud of his great life accomplishments with her and their off springs. It seems that the battle for Bo Bo should have been won when he looks around at his financial statement, home, cars and more. Bo Bo is not content and this stuff is not enough. He does not know what contentment is and does not even entertain settling down. He looks at it as lust verses love. As long as he lives and takes care of you, he feels that he can lust after the lady of the night. In his mind this is just the way of men.

Sacrifice after sacrifice that has been made for the family, why can't Bo Bo act right? The drinking, the smoking, the women and all his toys are not enough. He has to constantly fill his lust. Although, you have accepted many parts of Bo Bo's madness, it does not hurt any less. Pleasuring Bo Bo beyond your own sexual comfort still is not enough for Bo Bo. If he wants to raise the stakes in the bedroom you raise it and that still does not keep him home. The episodes may slow down but it never appears to cease. He keeps you on and slows down only if it seems as you will leave. Bo Bo wants both parts of his life and not to have one part independent of the other. It does not seem as if a testimony ever comes because this storm does not appear to be passing. Sometimes the storm calms but you can still see the waves rippling. Any minor disturbance can stir up the winds and the storm will roar again. Bo Bo likes to argue and fight because the rage in him is inflamed. He wrestles with his unhappiness and lays it before your feet. Bo Bo's face shows his inter disturbance and the rage that flows from him cannot be contained. It is a cycle with him that seems to have no end.

Enduring is the state that we find ourselves in. Endurance with Bo Bo is true labor. The labor is harder than laboring with child for nineteen hours. The odds of God showing up after years of an uphill battle with Bo Bo seem slim. Has God really heard our prayers, one might ask? Can one tell that we have a Bo Bo at home and that he steps out on us?

Lock the doors and kick him out sounds like a good plan on most days. The appearance of having a sound relationship would unravel if you let him go, it would be on public display. The embarrassment, loneliness and shame would be too much to bear. Although, we can find the way to pleasure ourselves with the sinful sex toys the story would end and not happily ever after. Holding on to Bo Bo can create the illusion that there just maybe some hope that happily ever after exists. Removing Bo Bo from our lives can expose the fact that we have discord. Our lies come to the surface and everyone knows. You see, no person in a relationship sets out to play a part in a play but as the relationship progresses and dress rehearsal ends the truth is revealed. The show goes live. There is neither Take 2 nor Take 3 and you do not remember how to say CUT! The relationship issues with Bo Bo are revealed like Janet Jackson's breast on Super Bowl Sunday.

Decisions to go public were never a sista's intent but her business preceded her when Bo Bo is seen out and about. Bo Bo is not discrete in the streets. He thinks he is creeping but someone always sees him. The person that sees Bo Bo lurking may not reveal it to the wife but the undertone of knowing comes over to the wife loud and clear when in a room with others. It may be that extra stare and that extra quiet hello that is whispered or that slight reservation. The woman to woman intuition is a tale-tell sign. Sista, you are not alone because the woman that whispers the soft hello sees her reflection in your mirror because she has been there or is there now. The familiarity of the signs to her are identified because it can never be erased from her heart or head. It is like the day a loved one died and no matter how much death that is experienced, it does not hurt any less. The feeling may not be able to be expressed but it is ever so heavy and real. It penetrates you inside and shows in your eyes. Your eyes are often thought to be the window to your soul and therefore you are exposed.

Sista, you are not alone because one day you will become the matriarch of your family and you will be called Big Ma, Nana, Mother Dear, Ma Dear, Mother on the church mother's board, and even deaconess because Bo Bo now sits on the deacon board. Sista stand tall. You are not the cause of your pain. You are strong and resilient. It is not your fault. Tell another sista your story so she does not breed self hatred, unworthiness inside or discontentment from within. You do not want another sista developing low self esteem over something she has no control over. Help another sista through prayer, counsel and advice. Be a sista's mentor. Let another sista off the hook and let her know it happened to you. Tell her she is not the first and by statistics will not be the last. Empower her to free her mind and walk as the queen that she is.

Let her know of your story and the story of others. Let her know to rise above in her own right. Be a rock to her, a foundation for her to rebuild. Be a confidant to her, an example for her and above all be real to her. Let her know I am Big Ma now, but I was where you are now. Let her know that the pain has never died and the painful memories are often triggered. Let her know that her story was a trigger to share with her now. Let her know how to move on whether she stays with Bo Bo or leave. Leave her with Sista you are not alone.

Chapter Seven

Is this your story?

*I*s this your story?

Woman A

Woman A grows up with her husband and lost her virginity to him. She was dedicated and faithful to him. He was her first and last man to the present time. She was raised not to be promiscuous but to be a good girl. Although, Bo Bo got caught cheating once, he convinces his wife that there will be no more. The Bo Bo in her life states there is a difference between lust and love. He states his lust and conquering other women in bed should not be confused with who he really loves. Woman A does not want Bo Bo to wander and tries to justify that he is not cheating by snooping in his phone and blackberry. While snooping she finds clues but the trail grows cold and she reasons that he could not be having an affair even though she finds names and numbers. Woman A does not want to be a victim again. She hurts badly and tells her story to anyone who listens. She asks older men that flirt with her about their Bo Bo behavior. Their advice is that yes, we all cheat and it is all right. They reveal that if your man is good you will never know because it does not take all night. They explain that when they cheat they treat the wife better. Let your man cheat in peace because you will have household peace in the long run. Woman A spirit is not rested and cannot accept that she is a victim of Bo Bo's deceit. She just exists in the moments of her marriage. She is very uneasy and waiting for Bo Bo to mess up so she can justify her leaving him with no uncertainties or any regrets this time. She regrets not leaving years ago when she had proof of his infidelity.

Woman B

Woman B has children from a previous relationship and has moved on to the next Bo Bo. She endures his affairs because she has tried many others and it is the same but at least this one provides for her and her children that are not his. She wants to leave him but stays because she does not believe it will be better with the next. She suffers silently and dies everyday. This Bo Bo will not marry her and makes it real clear that this is not an option for him. He says take me or leave me. He tells her you are the main one that I live with, five out of seven days. The other women in his life respect her and know that he is not faithful. The women respect their place and also respect woman B as being primary. They understand that their needs are not taken care of until woman B has been accommodated. Woman B is taken care of first. Woman B has never been married and desires to be but Bo Bo is not committing and years are passing her by. She wants to jump off his love ship and find another viable option. She believes that all men do the same thing which is why she appears to be stuck.

Woman C

Woman C has a Bo Bo that seems nerdy when it comes to the world of women. He is an Electrical engineer and not attractive. He is arrogant because of his financial status. He treats his woman C like hired help and he wants her to bow down at his throne. Women C is from the south and has been trained culturally to respect and keep her mate at all cost. She is the walking dead. She is always last and Bo Bo treats her bad but insists that through his accomplishments she should be grateful. He reminds her that many women would want to take her place and be a kept woman.

He fools around with another engineer on the job who is married as well. He takes his wife to all the social functions and also entertains his lover and her husband at his table at corporate events. He enjoys strip clubs while his wife is not allowed to go out and socialize in any manner unless he is in attendance. She stays home isolated from her extended family and friends because he insists that she has no life except the one he provides. Woman C inwardly hates him and wants to walk off so she can be free but she thinks of her children's welfare. Woman C believes that surely another man would appreciate a fraction of the worship and servicing that she does to her King Bo Bo in her life.

Woman D

Woman D is of small stature and sophisticated. She is the full package. She stops men in their tracks. She makes men want to serenade her. The attention that she gets is unbelievable. She loves the attention and the opportunity to sleep with different men. She is a loose woman because she feels as if she has been pushed into that life style because her Bo Bo is not faithful. She is married to the Bo Bo in her life but as fine as she is and as sophisticated as she may be it does not stop Bo Bo. She will perform any sex act for her man. She looks good and smells good. She cannot keep her Bo Bo satisfied. She thrives on the attention in the streets. She is with a famous gospel act and sleeps with the star of the group, owner of the business, stage manager, the pianist and other men in the gospel act. She has married men that do explicit acts of oral sex and other wild things even though they go home to there wife every night. Her purpose is not to hurt the wife but she says that men cheat so why shouldn't women. She would love her Bo Bo to give up his night life but she understands that this is not her reality. Woman D is beautiful and sexual and she still cannot master the Bo Bo in her life but she plays with any Bo Bo that likes her for the moment.

Woman E

Woman E is a devoted Christian and her husband is a preacher. Oh, yes, her Bo Bo is a preacher man. He also owns a small business and has finally yielded to sleeping with the secretary. The secretary has been after the reverend for years. His wife always noticed that the secretary had a thing for him at the company functions. The secretary's feelings were so strong you could cut it out with a knife in mid air.

The Christian couple was dedicated to church and their family.

They practiced bringing the family up in the Word of the almighty God. The reverend was trying his best not to be a Bo Bo because he wore the holy cloth but sister secretary has disrobed him and he got her pregnant. Yes, the secretary is pregnant by Reverend Bo Bo. She saw how well the reverend's wife lived therefore she wanted a fragment of her lifestyle even if she could not bear his name because of his wife.

Of course, nothing done in the dark is ever concealed permanently. The baby boy was born and given the reverend's name because the court served him with child support papers while he was with his wife and family on the church lawn after Sunday service. The clerk said loud and clearly "you have been served." His wife froze even though she was greeting the congregation as they went to their cars. Is this your story? Did you give your life to the Lord and thought that you were excluded from the typical Bo Bo madness, only to find out that the church building could not protect you. The first lady of Bo Bo stayed with him but she resented the ground that he walked on. She lost something that she has never found again all in the name of Bo Bo. It sickens her to know that a child was conceived by another while married to her husband. Reverend made a promise never to breathe that child's existence again. Even though it is unspoken it is ever so loud in his wife's ear.

Woman F

Woman F is unsaved and so is her spouse. They live day to day with no real purpose. The both are alcoholics and raising their children to do the same. The husband feels that his wife should be grateful because he is gainfully employed though the state and she has a job with the U.S. government. Her husband does not rave over her, she is his wife not to adore but they are equal partners in a marriage. Each spouse has to contribute 50/50. The husband never buys her any fine things or ravishes her as a woman. The Bo Bo in her life is in his early 60's. He loves the bar scene as old as he is. He loves the ladies in the streets. He treats them nicely and says kind words to them as well. He shows the ladies in the street lustful affection. He will spend his money on the women in the tavern without hesitation. He drinks so much that DUI's or DWI's should be apart of his name.

The wife patiently awaits his arrival from his nights out at the bar while playing solitaire. She is too embarrassed to go to the tavern to see if he is alright because she does not know which lady would be in his face tonight. She hopes he makes it home. The state job that he has requires that he keeps his driver's license. The wife is in between a rock and a hard place. Her Bo Bo cheats in the streets and stumbles home. He has done this for years and she tries to suppress the reality of it. She believes that this is how men are and that some people do not have a husband at all. She is old school and very private. She thinks that he has a good job and pays half on the bills. He was a good dictator over the children, so she just ENDURED. She keeps her secrets and suffers silently even though the world can see her story crystal clear. She wears the outward appearance for people but through her eyes you can see her turmoil.

Woman G

Woman G married an older illegal immigrant for money. She is so delighted to have him. In private, I asked her why did you marry this man and she replied, Big Ma got tired of sleeping with other people's husband, honey. Shocking expressions came over me and consumed my soul with a piercing tremble. With shock and disbelief, did Big Ma just say that? She is in her seventies and he is bordering ninety? Her response was so disturbing and unexpected it floored me and sent the alarms off. She said that she had four children by four different men and none was ever her husband. She said when the opportunity came along; she took that chance to become a wife. She said all my life I dated married men and I married this old man not really for the money but to have a husband of my very own. This was so sad to me to hear her pain.

How could woman G live with this kind of Bo Bo in her life? Why, would she accept so little? Wow, she left me stunned to know that she had such a story. While saddened with the Bo Bo experience that I had encountered her story tore more out of me. She really endured pain and a heavy burden from her experience. After she shared her story I felt some of her pain release even though she told the story in still and gentle whispers.

Chapter *Eight*

HELP ME HOLY SPIRIT!

*D*ear Holy Spirit,

Today is a new day but it has an old feel to it. I want to open up and let my guard down but it is hard. It seems as if life is moving but I am stuck in the same place. I am trying to find ways to keep my mind distracted. I woke up this morning and read the daily bread as I always do. When I read it and meditate on God's Word it feels as if I can really do it. I am trying to learn how to put one foot in front of the other and it seems I fall every time. If I fall is it that Bo Bo who trips me or do I allow him to trip me? In the back of my mind is my life's problem and Bo Bo is a big part of my hesitation and devastation. How can I suppress my feelings for the day? It is apparent that I have more questions than answers. I thought I would write you today in hopes that I can make it through after releasing some of my negative energy with this pen and paper. Why does this burden seem so heavy and that no one can seem to help me carry it? Here I go again, I will end for now.

Signed, *Heavy Burden*

*D*ear Holy Spirit,

I cannot bring myself to read another word from the Bible because it feels as if I am Job and I want to know why the Lord has forsaken me. Bo Bo stayed out late on Thursday night and then he came in the house and slept in the guest room. What is it now? Okay, I went to ask him what was up with his behavior and he said nothing. He had a sick look on his face and it gave me the creeps. I waited thirty minutes until he fell asleep and found a new number in his pager. I decided to copy that number as well as others down. I did not have the nerves to call them. I looked at the clock and it was 4:40 a.m. and I have to be at work at 7:00 a.m. What do I do? I went to work and time passed by slowly. I kept thinking of the numbers that I had jotted down from the pager. I decided to call the recent one. Wow, I called and the first thing that came out of my mouth is "Are you sleeping with my husband" which I called by name and she said "Yes". I immediately left the office and drove home to kill my husband. He denied everything. He said that was a old friend and he had some coupons for Dunkin Donuts in his car and when he saw her he gave them to her for her five kids. He said the coupons were in his car and that is how she knew what was in our car. The lady stated that she had sex with him in the car but he denied that. Later, after weeks of badgering he confesses to not having sex with her but that she performed a sex act on him. Holy Spirit, should I throw the marriage out the door? I did have sense enough to call the doctors office and make an appointment for him to get a HIV Aids Test. Holy Spirit, I do not hear you, are you there, let something fall off the counter for a sign that heaven exists.

Signed, *To Murder or Forgive*

*D*ear Holy Spirit,

Why does it seem as if my husband's wrath is directed solely at me? Is it because he is insecure or because I am not mature enough to keep quiet when he is angered. Holy Spirit, why does it seem as if I have no calming power when it comes to my man? Are we emotionally disconnected and we stay for the convenience of the family or does he want to leave me for the idea that the grass is greener on the other side. I feel the turmoil and stress and no matter what I do he is never content. Holy Spirit, is life meant to be complicated and have so many ups and downs? Should I move on to another relationship or is this really the way life works. I am so confused beyond measures that I feel that I am going insane. Is life meant to have these twists and turns that leads me to battle every time that I think the war is over? Waving the white flag is no problem for me because I want to surrender from the life of misery. Although, I wave the flag, no concession is accepted of my apparent defeat. Holy Spirit, the idea of you is my only source of comfort. I trust that you will not fail me as my bedmate does on any given night. I trust that there is light at the end of my tunnel too. If there is no light, please let me know so I can stop expecting that the unexpected is going to shed some light on my situation.

Good night my Holy One, give me peace for the moment and let me toss less this beautiful night.

Chapter Nine

My violations; His victories

*I*t feels as if Bo Bo's violations of women are accepted throughout society and the reason is that it is men's nature. It could be his natural nature but what about the nature of the beast theory. We train animals and mammals nationwide to get different behavior out of them. There's another saying you cannot teach a dog new tricks, a trainer can and does. Are women training men how to treat us? The fact that Bo Bo violates women and brags about it make him feels victorious. There is no hit on his hand for sharing his nightly mischief or extra curriculum activities with other women even though he has a wife. Men for years have kept the score to equate the value of their manhood. Their mere victory shows that women have suffered. It seems as if women play the part of the trash collector for men. It is hard to rid her of the awful dead smell that dwells inside of her. In order for the smell or stitch to go away first the trash has to stop coming her way so the odor will dissipate. Meeting Bo Bo after Bo Bo will leave ratchet foulness in her skin that she can taste through her mouth.

Accepting negative behavior should not be encouraged by society nor accepted. It should be frowned upon like teen pregnancy in the sanctified church or from the old school culture. Accepting Bo Bo's violations leave room for more and comfortably so. The new school woman says today that there is no need for marriage. They believe they can secure a financial future without a Bo Bo and have children through sperm donations. The value of a husband has hit rock bottom. A few women like the idea of marriage from the Cinderella fairy tale perspective. They just want to experience the ceremony and the feelings that go along with that big day of outwardly displaying love and affection. They want what the idea of marriage represents.

Women that can secure a sound financial life have found the value of men low on the totem pole. Most women do not want the burden of what men represent. They want the fairy tale but it truly does not work like that because Bo Bo is not programmed. Although, I am willing to believe if one could create a robot model of men in the flesh the value of stocks on wall street would bring the Dow Jones to a new high. Since women are big consumers this would make the USA richer three times over. A woman's fear of failure and being violated would be over. She would be free to love without conditions. She would be able to have a voice and a choice. What a victory for her and him. The fear of heart break and games removed would embark on a life of personal security for the woman. Bo Bo would not be left out because the queen that he has can deliver if given fair playing ground. Keep in mind man was created first but still needed a help mate. The victory would be a win/win and not a concession with the woman always waving the white flag because the vows are broken by Bo Bo.

His victories outside the home counteract her empowerment. Violating women take them out of there comfort zone. It places many guarded barriers, it raises constant suspicion and breeds discontentment. Women's emotions are half the battle. Knowing that she does not have to fight with Bo Bo over his heart at the expense of her sanity is plain old liberating. Let freedom ring, would have new meaning.

Chapter *Ten*

STOP CELL PHONE CHECKING AND DRIVE BYS

Stop cell phone checking and the drive bys that occupy your time and mind with unhealthy energy. Mastering Perry Mason and Johnnie Cochran skills should be saved for something else other than monitoring Bo Bo. Monitoring Bo Bo's activity does not change what he does, only how he does it. If you have the bold Bo Bo, he changes how he does it. Playing the private eye helps you doubt and beat up on yourself. It consumes you inside and out. It unravels threads that are useless because you cannot pull it apart. The threads turn into a spider web mess. The more you unravel the harder it is to untangle and it frustrates you and wear you out emotionally. Go get some thread and start to unravel it and let it fall where it may and try to sort through it and see what it becomes. If you did that you will see that it would be best to throw that spool out and get a new one. I wish that life would be that cut and dry where you could just throw Bo Bo out. Chances are the next spool will be a bigger mess.

Sad but true, the new spool may spin out of control without you ever touching it. Picture that. Life is uncertain and the possibilities seem to dwindle down as time goes by. In no time at all you turn into Big Ma and make it through because time passed. Reality is a dose of medicine and the cure seems to have no existence. When you move about in life doing what your obligations are you never forget that the inner you has a weight that no one else can see. If you inspected your life, it would force you to look in your own mirror that has been safely tucked away. You carefully wrap it from breaking while out of sight because you do not want to break it. The breakage would mean seven years of bad luck and with your current condition who could afford that.

Pressing forward is a must and not debatable because others are dependent on you. Checking behind Bo Bo only hinders you from completing the daily required task. It feels as if you drink the deadly poison for Bo Bo when he should bear his own issues. Carrying around

Bo Bo's issues will cause you to sink and become depressed beyond reasons. The stress is not worth you creating health problems for yourself. Stress can bring on many evils that can work against your body, mind and soul. As we have discussed Bo Bo is not whole and people who are wounded can only wound. Think about how you can bring healing if you are lamed and mane. It is like that cousin who borrows from everyone saying, "I will pay you back" and you believe them. You know they owe everyone including you but their game is so tight that you have been suckered yet again. When the money leaves your pocket you have an epiphany and say "what the heck was I thinking".

Apply the "cousin borrowing" theory to Bo Bo and know that because of your love for him he can make you love him in that moment and the epiphany keeps coming. He really does not love you or he does not know what love is. Love is not hurting others. Love is not lying and taking advantage of you because he knows that you love him and are committed to him. Love is not taking you for granted over and over again. Love should make him change and not violate you whether you are present or not. Love would allow him to tell other ladies I am taken with his expressions and demeanor. He should not show sign that he is in the market for another in no kind of way. He should not flirt in a lustful way with others out of respect for his significant other. Another woman's advance should be shot down quickly because his mind is on another level.

You would think that some women seeing Bo Bo with a ring on his finger would turn them off but it does not. Some women told me those are the ones that they gravitate to. They do not feel insulted or offended. They would rather him be married. They only want to play and not do the labor of love thing that the wife does. They say that when Bo Bo comes by his clothes are clean, his socks are mended, his bills are paid and they can reap the benefits of his allowance. They like to relax and fulfill their fantasies with him in the presence of no children and no aroma of a meal that they had to prepare for him. Being with a man with the ring on his finger represents a peace of mind.

The wife does all the work in the trenches for Bo Bo and provides the support that he needs and he shares the best of him outside of the home with Ms. Ready. She can be ready at any given time because she has no responsibility in the challenging role of family. She can text him throughout the day and call him on his cell to see when he is ready to play. Then she sends him home to the wife to run his bath water, wash his clothes, rob Peter to pay Paul with the bills and have a short temper with her and the kids because he had more peace with Ms. Ready.

Checking the cell and pager makes him stay out later and use the excuse "since you are accusing me, I do not want to come home to the aggravation". Bo Bo creates an environment and cannot dwell in his own creation nor does he take responsibility. He runs out and lay with Ms. Ready for peace. The wife is dwelling with everything but peace. It does not benefit the wife to make the discovery and perpetuate a cycle that does not stop.

The wife has had choices placed on her that she did not opt for. Consequentially, the choices hurt her when her goal was only to love. Her heart kept her there and before she knew it, she became Big Ma. Bo Bo cannot perform in bed any longer because he is impotent. Now, the aged Bo Bo stays home and tells the world that he loves his wife. He forgets that he dogged her into a state that words could not express. She wanted a monogamous man and family. She wanted the happily ever after that she read about. The wife's journey did not lead her down the happily ever after path but she settled for one reason or the other. She had to weigh out the pros and cons of their relationship. It leaned in Bo Bo's favor by a margin of slim to very slim.

In all reality, checking after Bo Bo is not a good idea unless you are willing to end the relationship upon discovery. The pains of finding out about indiscretions are overwhelming. It does not provide a solution and it does not bring the indiscretion to an end. It is more baggage for you to carry. You are already overloaded. You are reeking with a foul odor from Bo Bo's garbage, already. You let the world encourage you to stay because they believe in "thick and thin" and "for better and for worst".

Chapter Eleven

Breaking Away from Bo Bo

$\mathcal{B}$reaking away from Bo Bo is not easy. The reason that Bo Bo exists in your life, after all of the heart aches, headaches and drama is senseless in itself. Therefore, addressing issues of breaking away from him is challenging in many regards. The wife wants Bo Bo to exist in her life but she wants him to be an improved model.

The fact is that your mind says that the relationship is hopeless and your heart holds on to hope. Years has rolled by, your tears has made a river. Fears have kept you with him and breaking away would be your deliverance. The deliverance is viewed as a peace of mind and a reward but it comes with a tremendous price. The price feels like your flesh is being eaten at while alive. The process is slow. The speed of the process is at a snail pace. It seems that the good things that Bo Bo has done moves few and far between. The victories in the relationship are well noted and memorable. The record shows why one stays with Bo Bo after so many losses.

The losses are so frequent that no record has to be recorded because it is sure to surface again. Arriving at the decision to break away was a major ordeal in itself because anticipating the loss comes with pain. Most women are guided through life by emotions. Emotions take a life of their own. Emotions of a woman, good or bad, constitutes where she is at that time in her life. Emotions are not factual but it is the position where the woman's feelings take her. The emotions of a woman could allow her to feel the hurt. Also, the hurting and the healing process could occur simultaneously for women. She has that ability to multi task; this is the gift that the female possesses.

Breaking away from Bo Bo does not seem as an option for women but it is an unwanted necessity that must be addressed before further insanity or ill behavior is produced. A woman was designed by God to be a help mate and a complete a man; therefore execution in any situation is her true calling. Women do not want to stand alone without a Bo Bo but she wants to instinctively help, repair, mend, assist and complete him. Women are no stranger to self sacrificing. She is a nurturer and a problem solver by design. Now, to break away from her quest to be Bo Bo's soul mate and his completer is a great task of burdens. She wants a man that loves her and is committed to her without feeling expendable at any given time. By society standards, Bo Bo is not expected to be faithful and content. It is said that men can have a healthy appetite for women and the lust thereof.

Escaping from Bo Bo may feel liberating and also have feelings of bondage as well. To escape is the act of separating. The relationship has created so much pain because of Bo Bo's inability to give his all to the relationship and not step outside of it is complex for him. A part of the bondage is being separated from him, while it may be best mentally; it creates an emotional roller coaster. It can take you up as fast as it takes you down. Breaking away from Bo Bo for most women is not that cut and dry. When the cord is cut from Bo Bo then the process of healing should begin. The process can be very painful when the end was not your decision. It is a forced choice. A forced choice takes time to accept and move toward resolution.

A forced choice is out of necessity and the choice has to be made against the odds. Most women feel regret and doubt when they have to choose to leave. The realization is that he will never leave or stop sleeping with you because having several women is who he is. If a person has diabetes they would have to watch, monitor and control their sugar intake. This would not be an easy task for someone who likes sweets and does not want to set limits to keep their diabetes under control. The fact is that a diabetic has to take control; otherwise it can result in death. If a woman does not take control of an unhealthy relationship that keeps her stressed out and emotionally drained, it can result in premature death. Being stressed out is not good, it works on the body as well as the mind.

Rarely does one understand what they have in a relationship until they are on the outside looking in. The relationship with Bo Bo should not seem as a life of imprisonment. It is a relationship that two enter into freely. Formal relationship training should be mandatory in order to start a relationship. The Bo Bo's of life does not come with warning signs. There is no early indication. You have no idea that they are crazy, broken and has no desire to be repaired.

The challenge is to find a peaceful place within you when all Bo Bo's hell is raging around you. All battered women do not leave because life has their factors. I am not advocating staying in harms way, but many of us do. Harm could be verbal, physical or psychological. Infidelity, disrespect and lying are abuse as well. The fact is all relationships have some issues. There are different degrees of issues but none should cross the fine line of abuse.

We have to stand up and say to Big Ma that the secret of Bo Bo is being revealed. How many years have you been married is not the victory, if it was filled with more tears than joy. Peace of mind is the prize and it is immeasurable. Your mind has to be free and know that happiness is a choice. You need to choose happiness. Your happiness should be so radiant that it spreads like a contagious virus. If you are miserable in a relationship with Bo Bo take ownership of it. You have to decide that changes need to take place. The change should not be his choice but a necessity for you.

Pray about it, give it to God, and above all trust him to work it out. This might mean that it is best to go separate ways. It is OK to stand alone and have your own family. Relationships should not self inflicted hardship. Suffering is not necessary or positive in a relationship. Self infliction occurs when you are allowed to be abused and/or victimized in the name of love. Think about love; cheating, hurt and pain are not in the same category. Glitter does not equal gold. There is a difference between good and bad times in a relationship. Bad times should not mean to act uneducated nor ignorant. Bad times do not mean infidelity. Bad times do not mean some one going up side of your head. Bad times do not mean substance abuse or an addiction that destroys people lives around you. Bad times do not mean feeling bad and having someone call you anything other than your name.

Respecting each other and the commitment is the goal of the relationship. Remember if your Bo Bo is a snake, he will bite every time. Snake behavior does not change. God is the only one who can change people. Please note that God does not change anyone against their will.

Escaping Bo Bo can come through a physical separation of severing the relationship. Or it can come mentally when one has zoned out and becomes numb to ill treatment. If one decides to stay, stop participating in Bo Bo's madness. Do not let what he does move or shake you anyway. Do not give your energy and power to someone who wants to self destruct themselves. We all know that some stay for the children and some stay because of "LOVE". Some stay for the drama factor "because woe is me" is the ones who love sympathy. Some stay out of fear because they are afraid of the unknown.

Ladies, pick your position and stand firmly in the confidence to know that you are great and can master Bo Bo one way or the other. Choose your position and accept the peace. It will be priceless whether he changes or not. Let nature take its course. Imagine flying as the prettiest dove with the right attitude on a good day, with great weather. Picture yourself swimming in the blue waters that look like the blue crayon that melted from the Crayola Box. See yourself, lying flat on your back and the waves are carrying you. You feel great and royal.

Escape my sista one way or another. No one can quench your thoughts nor think for you. See the vision of yourself and have the power to have greatness and peace because God said so. Remember, even Bo

Bo is not too hard for God but he has to want the peace for himself. Meanwhile, I say to you to fly, soar and ride the wave of life to escape from captivity, depression and drama. Take your place on the throne; it has your name on it:

Your Highness
Queen
Princess
Lady
Majesty

Chapter Twelve

Adjustment/Alignment

Learn the lesson from Big Ma and the others around. Do not experience a bad relationship because the knowledge is there. If the pit falls of a relationship exist, adjust and align them. Gaining knowledge helps avoid repeated judgment issues. My grandmother always told me to listen and learn as not to fall in every hole. She told me to trust her and know that there are many holes and by listening to her I could avoid them. Sista's see the holes; do not fall in them again, please. Do not let more of your life elapse on things that does not enhance you. If you are in the hole, you can fill it in and walk over it. The patch will represent that you have grown.

For many women we feel that we are Cinderella and we married the best candidate available at the time. We picked out a Bo Bo that has some good qualities and potential. We try to clean up the rest. The realization is that life does not work that way. It comes down to **"What's your woman's worth?"** Decide to adopt a new perspective on life and focus on the three P's: Peace, Positivity and Prosperity. It is important to know that no human being can bring you happiness. Decide to be happy. It is just that **S I M P L E.**

Meditate and practice being happy. Find ways to bring your spirit up and keep it up. Believe that God hears you and has given you the power. Know that you are a spirit and you have purpose. If you are not focused it leads to a life of drama and confusion. Know that anything not like God is the opposite of his agenda. Know that Satan is real and has a strategy to keep us down and living in chaos. How does confusion and drama work? Through people which are not working for God but against him.

Life is short and guess what, it is! Reflect on your love ones that have preceded you in death and see that life is short. Use this moment to be happy and free. Know that Bo Bo is not all to life. Know that his mistress is not all to life. Know that his self destructive behavior will not go unpunished. Know that his infidelity is not against you, it is against himself. It really comes down to his self worth. Keep in mind that a woman's worth is priceless. There is no need to compromise your value.

Trying to be all to Bo Bo will not change him. Fill yourself up with positivity, it will give you peace. Fill yourself up until you overflow. Help others with no resentment neither envy but with good cheer. Help yourself and then help others.

Be liberated in your situation and it will not depress or stress you. The strategy lies within you. A key point to remember is that human beings act out their issues. Do not let anyone cause you destruction, guard your heart. God says when someone wrongs you he will make them a footstool for you to rest on them.

Bo Bo not doing right will not go unchecked. A cheating man **"ALWAYS GETS CAUGHT"**. They are broken and want to be exposed in order to get deliverance but go about things the wrong way. The male ego is not any help either.

Do know that what you go through with Bo Bo is not new nor should it be acceptable. When women stop letting the Bo Bo's do what they want, it will stop. They cannot cheat alone. Then we can put the woman's worth on the stock market and use our lessons learned to have a strategy to cease Bo Bo's abuse of females.

The question is asked "how can you stop Bo Bo's madness?" Close your legs to other people's man and buy your own gym shoes. If you are a SheNeeda and you did not have a father, stop having a pity party and tell Bo Bo to go home to his wife. If Bo Bo is turned down he cannot act out alone. Who wants to start the process? Who wants to stop fulfilling their personal needs and stop the booty call first?

It should be all of us because we know how the cycle works. We have either experienced being violated by a man first or second hand. When the Nay Nay's and the SheNeeda's clean up their act and leave other people's husbands alone they will not have to worry. When they get a husband the karma will not have to come back on them. When they settle down they can have peace.

Men can act like children; they do what we let them get away with. Let's decide today no more. Let's watch our woman's worth go up and burst at the stock market seams. Let's take our families back one Bo Bo at a time. If Bo Bo cannot comply and play by the rules then he plays alone. Let's remember men are not our completer. It is not mandatory that we marry.

The dream has been sold to us in many fairy tales. In those stories they never stated drama or that Bo Bo has Cinderella and Snow White at the same time. It did not say that the old lady in the shoe had five baby Daddies and Bo Bo was one of them. Create your own story and start by working on you before connecting with anyone. Also, if you have already connected and have a family it is not too late. You can come up with a new game plan and an effective strategy and it can work. You can educate yourself even if you have to drop the "R" in **Mrs. Used** and become **Ms. Possibilities.** Fill yourself up with good things tell Bo Bo no more now, either he will comply or he can fly. Keep this in mind because you and Bo Bo have the same address, you do not have to accept abuse in the name of love. Freedom is in your mind. Start writing in a journal today and explore what brings you joy. When you find joy take it in and enjoy it to the fullest extent. Then exhale and inhale some more of the joy.

Lift your head up high and know that you are the completer but you cannot complete someone who is broken or cheats. Create different mindsets, goals and expectations. List your goals for yourself and participate with the Bo Bo that wants to stay faithful, loyal, committed and dedicated to you. Let go of the past. Today is your day and opportunity to write your happily ever after with or without a Bo Bo in your life.

Dream, imagine and be child like. Pretend that you are happy until you reach the pinnacle of joy. You can make a positive impact while completing your journey through this moment in time. Be prayerful, be peaceful, be positive, be prosperous, and be bold with your Bo Bo. Watch how your joy unfolds in life. Take a stand today and know that drama should not exist as your reality when it comes to unfaithfulness, abuse and lack of respect.

Change is now, change is you and you are CHANGED. Now live happily ever after because it is what you decide to make it.

Chapter *Thirteen*

SISTA SOAR AND CHANGE YOU!!!

*A*pply the lessons learned, after hiding and crying alone, and start to soar, my Sista. Soaring is an elevation. You may not hit the ground running but at least you hit the ground. After reading this book, lift your head and start your elevation process. Let your head go down when praying and reading. Never let your head hang down regarding a man or a Bo Bo in your life. Lift your head to address what issue may arise because you can look it in the eye and begin to learn a strategy to operate and work your way through the presence. Stand in the presence and demand that it manifest positive things for you. Let those experiences shape you into something refined, priceless and beautiful.

Let your new manifestation yield an attitude of contentment and satisfaction. You are what God created and are wonderful. It is not too late to start anew and fresh life. Let your new attitude govern how you fly whether it is at a low or high altitude. Open your eyes and mouth and let beauty generate. Let the new eyes of your soul be bold and piercing to show your joy. Seize the moment and capitalize because it is your season. A season of grace, expectations and achievements is what life is about. It is a season to realize that you cannot change people, only God can. You cannot change what people do. You can remove yourself from their path, so the negativity does not affect you. Learn not to major in the minors. Learn that life has minors and that you do not let it become a major for you.

Do not become a trash receptacle for anyone because your garbage pick up is once a week and not everyday. You have no accommodation for trash that exceeds your limits. Do know that snakes are snakes and they will bite. A snake will gravitate and operate by its nature to bite. It may appear that it will not but it will. Never get confused and befriend the snake unless you do not mind the bite. The bite may kill you. You must know what risks you are willing to take. You have to do the damage control for yourself. Self preservation has to be a priority for you. You need to know your limits especially if you have dependents that depend on you. If you compromise yourself, you risk the dependents as causalities. If you allow a male child to witness you being abused by Bo Bo, he can grow up to keep Bo Bo's madness going strong. He needs to see correction and zero tolerance to abusive behavior. There is a difference between spats and abuse. Spats have rules and abuse has no rules and will spin out of control.

Set boundaries for yourself and stick to them. Do not let life deal you any hand and you play anyway. Know that you have choices and life can work. It can be favorable and rewarding because you deserve it. Do not paint a picture of hopelessness. Do not let someone else use your canvas and paint a picture of your life for you. Everyone's perception of life is different. The way you deal with your life and the interpretation of your experiences are personal. No one can live peacefully for you that an individual choice.

Many people are visionless and pessimistic. I call them dream killers. The best person to dream for you is YOU. People paint the picture of their life with their Bo Bo more wholesome than it is really. Their selective memory does not show the despair that they feel more times than not.

Know that the path of life is not a guided tour on a vacation. The path may take you in many directions. The choices at times may seem damning one way or the other. It is fair to say that we should not allow our poor choices to feel as if change is not possible. Position yourself to win and learn while traveling the life's journey. You should find purpose then your possibilities can exceed your greatest expectation. Know that destructive people or relationships cannot destroy you unless you allow it. Cutting losses early in a negative relationship is a good choice because you can free yourself to move into a new direction faster. Welcome peace early and it will only enhance your life.

Life does not come with a manual but you can live to see that behavior and choices yield certain results. It doesn't take a rocket scientist to figure out that love and pain is not healthy together. Pain is not encouraging. It should not be the way of life. You may encounter some

Bo Bos but make a clear choice and remember to make it early. In life there are many holes and pitfalls, you do not have to fall into everyone. Let wisdom help you.

Chapter *Fourteen*

Understand and forge ahead, Create the New

Lack of understanding and knowledge can bring out despair in you. When we are not informed it can keep us discouraged. After reading this book, you should see a common thread of women. You can begin to build a new foundation that promotes healthy growth. You should not blame anyone else for your state of being after today. You are accountable for the here and now. You have explored what you are up against when it comes to the Bo Bo's of the world. You know that this is common and that the behavior you are against does not have to swallow you up alive.

Understand that you got in that relationship by not knowing and by trying to love. You got there as a natural progression of a relationship. No one intends to get lost but somehow it happens. No one purposefully set out to be abused or misused. Life can spin out of control until you end up at an unfamiliar place. No one is to blame but the reality is that change needs to occur.

The questioning processes lead you to the beginning of time. It went back to the Garden of Eden. It started with the first woman and man of the universe. You have tried to sort things out from the beginning. You were looking to see how you ended up here. A valid explanation is that the initial sin of mankind landed you there. The broken relationship happened in the Garden. The sin in the garden is real. Tracing your past may help you change. Never regret and dwell on the past mistakes. The past has shaped you into the beauty that you are currently.

It was okay to ask the question, who wanted Bo Bo anyway. It is clear that you are in a relationship with him and he is not fulfilling his end of the monogamous relationship. His short comings and secrets are clear. You just wanted to know who wants a fragment of your man. You wanted to know if he treated her the same way or if it was just you. You have found that the brokenness was not only him. You had to have broken expectations to accept his disrespect as well. Bo Bo cheating and exploring with other women was bold. It was clear that he was broken and that society accepts it as "he's just a M A N."

After going through the hurt and pain you came to the point that you wanted some revenge. You did not want to wait on God; you wanted to self inflict him with the best revenge that you could conger up. You wanted to feel beautiful and desired by another man. You wanted to cheat and show Bo Bo that he should want to do right by you. You wanted him to know that you are marketable. You came to the realization that you could not make him pay. You found that you could not lower your standards and values. The fact is that some payback was needed but it could not come at your hands. The law of nature has to pay him back.

After dealing with your emotions, it was good to know that you were not alone. It is a good thing to discover that this was not uniquely and exclusively a problem that fell on your door step. This has happened before and it is not a strike against you personally, it is what it is. Knowing you are not alone should help you gain strength. You can overcome anything.

The stories were shared to show different women experiences. This happens to the young and old. The stories let you know that the pain that you feel has been felt by others. It shows that there is really nothing new under the sun. It is apparent that the stories outnumber countless experiences of ups and downs with Bo Bo. The stories are real, utilize them as a guide. Do not focus on having a pity party. You can stop the "woe is me" and everyone else is happy. Everyone experiences something.

The Holy Spirit was a sounding board for you. You shared your emotions. You shared some of your feelings of your private thoughts. The diaries of women make the walls in the heart speak. They are loud and the chatter seems to have many voices that are hard to decipher.

The voices have much to tell. It sounds like an orchestra, a marching band and a church choir all performing simultaneously. Exploring the emotions through the diary shows that your feelings have credence.

His violation has caught up with him. Do not make his problems yours. This should not be an option. Bo Bo has been exposed. His games have been identified and his indiscretion is on public display. The element of surprise has been dispelled. Realize that the violation has occurred and move forward.

You are finding information that leads you to the other women. The women know that they are second or third fiddle and do not care. They have there own self-serving agenda which is good enough for them. When Bo Bo is found out, it fuels the alternate relationship. The drama of you chasing him down makes you look insane. Stop your private eye work. Keep yourself free of unnecessary bondage that you cannot bear.

Breaking away from Bo Bo could come in different ways. It can come as a mental or physical freedom. Once, you have peace of mind you can begin to explore what option is best for you. It could be to stay or leave. You need to understand that a change needs to occur. Separating the physical will not take him out of your system. The separation is to gain the peace while working through the process. It will start you on a new journey.

Once, the peace is gained you can begin your adjustment and alignment period. Now, you should have a position. The position is to gain clarity and focus on what is important to you. It is a process that may not occur overnight. Many issues may have to be worked out. You can work them one by one. Work in peace because it is less strain. The alignment and adjustment may start small but it will yield freedom and encouragement. Keep moving in the right direction.

Sista, the change is beginning. You can say to each other, "Sista, soar and change. You are responsible for you and no one else." The change has to come from within and radiate outward. Conceive some better possibilities for yourself. Even though the progress may be small but it is measurable. The progress, great or small, should take form. You are in a different place which you never had the power to imagine. A spark has begun to flicker and you are suddenly combustible. You are setting everything in your path on fire. This shows that you have been there; the fire shows that you just left there. It also shows that the past created the fiery that you now have, the fire that illuminates you are ready to conquer a new outlook. You have grown. You are ready to share your light. Accept the fire and allowed it to resonate through you.

Understand how you are able to forge ahead and create anew. Create a new story, new vision and a story of change. You have clearly shown that the past can yield something new and positive. You can show that the Bo Bo's of life exist, but how you exist with them is a choice and not a life sentence. You have learned that you do not have to accept a relationship of pain. You have accepted this new change of life. You are walking in abundance. Christ wants you to have a full life. It is good to see your new and renewed faith. You are winning while creating the new. You are released to write your ending.

There is nothing perfect, stop looking! Marriage is not separate. Single is not lonely. God has left you a key. See what it opens. <u>**Do not settle just to have**</u> **"The Company of a MAN".**

The Company of A M A N

Some Women feel they need the company of a man
They take beatings, disrespect, broken hearts and unfinished dreams
Just for the company of a man

Some women bear children and struggle to raise them alone
Some loss sight of origin, dropping their once held high heads
Just for the company of a man

Some women allow their children to be raped and molested by their man
They will do jail time, deteriorate and die
Just for the company of a man

Some Women degrade themselves by being men sex slaves
They allow their insides to be destroyed from the sex abuse
Just for the company of a man

Have they ever stopped and dug deep into their souls
Who conceived man, who carried man, who gave birth to man, who raised man?

W O M A N
Wake up my, Sista